OCR Twenty First Century GCSE Chemistry Revision Plus
Workbook Answers
Author: Dorothy Warren

GW01288460

Page 4

1. a) Pollutants are chemicals that can harm the environment and our health. They enter the atmosphere as a result of human activity, e.g. burning fossil fuels.
 b) Sulfur dioxide can cause acid rain which has an impact on our food chain because the water in rivers and lakes becomes too acidic for plants and animals to survive. Natural resources like trees are also affected.
 c) i)–iii) Accept three of the following:
 Carbon dioxide – traps heat in Earth's atmosphere (greenhouse gas); nitrogen oxides – causes acid rain and causes breathing problems / can make asthma worse; carbon monoxide – displaces oxygen in the blood which can lead to death; sulfur dioxide – causes acid rain; particulates, e.g. carbon – make buildings dirty and can make asthma and other lung infections worse if inhaled.

2. a) i)–iv) In any order.
 i) Nitrogen.
 ii) Oxygen.
 iii) Argon and other noble gases.
 iv) Water vapour, carbon dioxide and other gases.
 b) i)–ii) In any order. i) Nitrogen, 78% **ii)** Oxygen, 21%

3. a) i) Concentrations of pollutants in the air.
 ii) It means that air quality can be assessed.
 b) It means that in every one million (1 000 000) molecules of air, 5 molecules will be carbon monoxide.

Page 5

1. Data can be used to test a theory or explanation.

2. a) i)–iii) In any order.
 i) Variables (i.e. factors that change) affect concentrations, e.g. volume of traffic, weather conditions.
 ii) Accuracy of measuring equipment.
 iii) User's skill in using the measuring equipment and in recording the data accurately.
 b) It will be somewhere between the top and bottom figures you have recorded.
 c) 0.3 in town centre data.
 d) The operator might have misread the scale.
 e) So that you can check that it is reliable – if you have lots of repeated measurements you can see more easily if one stands out.

Page 6

2. f) i) Mean = $\dfrac{\text{Sum of all values}}{\text{Number of values}}$

 ii) Outliers

 iii) Mean (town) = $\dfrac{2.5 + 3.0 + 3.5}{3}$ = 3ppm

 Mean (country) = $\dfrac{0.2 + 0.1 + 0.1 + 0.2}{4}$ = 0.15ppm

 iv) The mean sulfur particulates concentration is significantly higher in the town centre than in the country park.
 g) The amount of carbon monoxide particles are significantly higher in the city centre. The data supports the theory that sulfur particulates are an example of a pollutant caused by human activity.
 h) Yes. Because the difference between the mean values is a lot bigger than the range of each set of data. If the difference between the mean values had been smaller than the range there would have been no real difference. The result would have been insignificant and the data would not support the theory.

Page 7

1. a) Elements are the 'building blocks' of all materials.
 b) Tiny particles called atoms.

2. a) Al **b)** Fe **c)** K **d)** C **e)** O

3. a) Bigger 'building blocks'.
 b) A compound.
 c) One nitrogen atom and three hydrogen atoms.

4. a)–c) In any order.
 a) Joined atoms are s
 b) Separate atoms are
 c) Joined atoms are s different ways.

5. Reactants ⟶

6. a) i) Combustion is a chemical reaction which occurs
 burn, releasing energy as heat.

Page 8

6. a) ii) Oxygen.
 b) i) $C(g) + O_2(g) \longrightarrow CO_2(g)$
 ii) 1 carbon atom (solid) + 1 oxygen molecule (gas) ⟶ 1 molecule of carbon dioxide (gas)
 c) No atoms are lost or produced during a chemical reaction.

7. a)–c) Accept three of the following:
 Carbon dioxide – power station and exhaust emissions; nitrogen oxides – power station and exhaust emissions; sulfur dioxide – power station emissions; water vapour – exhaust emissions; carbon particulates – power station and exhaust emissions; carbon monoxide particles – exhaust emissions.

8. a) Hydrocarbon.
 b) i) Propane gas + Oxygen ⟶ Carbon dioxide + Water
 ii) When a hydrocarbon such as propane gas is burned in air, carbon dioxide and water (hydrogen oxide) is produced, resulting in complete combustion.

Page 9

9. a) i)–ii) In any order. i) Carbon particulates (C) **ii)** carbon monoxide (CO).
 b) i) Propane gas + Oxygen ⟶ Carbon particulates + Water
 Propane gas + Oxygen ⟶ Carbon monoxide + Water
 ii) Carbon particulates and carbon monoxide are in exhaust emissions and emissions from power stations – they cause breathing difficulties and have a big environmental impact.
 c) Sulfur + Oxygen ⟶ Sulfur dioxide gas

10. a) i) During the combustion of fuels, high temperatures can cause nitrogen in the atmosphere to react with oxygen and produce nitrogen monoxide.
 ii) $N_2(g) + O_2(g) \longrightarrow 2NO(g)$
 b) i) Nitrogen monoxide + Oxygen ⟶ Nitrogen dioxide
 ii) NOx

Page 10

1. a) Carbon particulates.
 b) Carbon dioxide is a greenhouse gas (traps heat in the atmosphere) so the annual rise in concentration is contributing to global warming. This is leading to climate change.
 c) Can be blown by the wind and reacts with water to produce acid rain.

Page 11

1. a) Pattern.
 b) i) Pollen in the air.
 ii) Hay fever.

2. a) There are lots of variables, e.g. temperature, humidity, other pollutants.
 b) i) Skin tests. Pollen was stuck to the skin of volunteers using plasters.
 ii) In some volunteers the skin had an allergic reaction. The results showed that people with a pollen allergy also suffered from hay fever. Those who did not have a pollen allergy did not suffer from hay fever.
 c) Other scientists studied the data and repeated the skin test experiments. The fact that the same results were always produced proved that they were reliable.

3. a) That although nitrogen oxide can increase the chance of an asthma attack, it is not the primary cause.
 b) i)–ii) In any order.
 i) What factors cause asthma.
 ii) What factors aggravate asthma.

Page 12

1. Because air pollution is everywhere and therefore affects everyone.

2. a) i) Electricity.
      ii) Sulfur dioxide, particulates.
      iii) Sulfur, natural gas, fuel oil.
      iv) Renewable, solar, wind, hydroelectric.
   b) i) Efficient, fuel.
      ii) Electricity.
      iii) Sulfur dioxide.
      iv) Biodiesel.
      v) Public transport.
      vi) Catalytic converters, carbon, nitrogen.

3. a) $CO(g) + O_2(g) \longrightarrow CO_2(g)$
   b) $2NO(g) + 2CO(g) \longrightarrow N_2(g) + 2CO_2(g)$

Page 13

1. People from many countries agreed to reduce carbon dioxide emissions and targets were set for individual countries. The governments of the countries agreed to take appropriate measures to meet the targets.

2. a) **i)–ii) In any order. Accept any other suitable answers.**
      i) Legal limits set for vehicle exhaust emissions, which are enforced by statutory MOT tests.
      ii) Catalytic converters were made compulsory on new vehicles.
   b) **i)–ii) In any order. Accept any other suitable answers.**
      i) MOT tests have had to be updated to deal with the legal limits set for vehicle exhausts.
      ii) When new cars / car parts are developed, the technology used has to meet all the new legal requirements.

3. **a)–c) In any order. Accept any other suitable answers.**
   a) Doorstep collections of paper, bottles, metals and plastics for recycling.
   b) Regular bus / train services.
   c) Park and ride schemes.

4. **a)–b) In any order. Accept any other suitable answers.**
   a) Turn the TV off and do not leave it on standby. This uses less energy and therefore reduces the demand for energy from power stations, which in turn reduces air pollution.
   b) Recycle paper, bottles, metals and plastics. This helps to conserve natural resources and also saves energy.

Page 14

1. a) Data.
   b) i) Atoms.
      ii) Water.
   c) i) Outlier.
      ii) Factors.
   d) i) Elements.
      ii) Formulae.
   e) i) Compounds.
      ii) Molecules.
      iii) True value.
   f) Correlation.
   g) Sulfur dioxide.
   h) Chemical reaction.

Page 15

2.

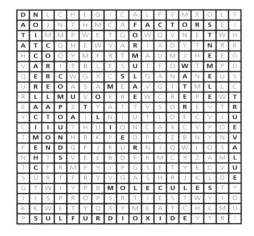

Page 16

1. a) **i)–ii) In any order. Accept any other suitable answers.**
      i) Material: Cotton. Obtained: Plant.
      ii) Material: Paper. Obtained: Wood.
   b) Synthetic materials.
   c) i) Chain molecules containing only hydrogen and carbon atoms.
      ii) Their molecular chains are of different lengths.

2. a) Soft b) Flexible / elastic c) Car tyres d) Conveyor belts
   e) Polythene f) Light g) Hard h) Water resistant
   i) Lightweight j) Waterproof k) Clothing l) Bottles.

Page 17

1. Because the properties of a product will affect how durable and effective it is as an end product.

2. a) i) Human error, e.g. the investigator wrote the measurement down incorrectly.
      ii) An outlier should be discounted.
   b) Calculate the mean flexibility.

3. a) Polymerisation is an important chemical process in which small hydrocarbon molecules, called monomers, are joined together to make long molecules called polymers.
   b) i)

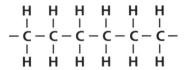

   ii) atoms; reactants.

Page 18

1. a) Wood b) Polychloroethene c) Unreactive d) Does not rot
   e) Carrier bags f) Ethene.

2. a) Rubber has a tangled mass of long-chain molecules. The atoms in each molecule are held together by strong covalent bonds, but there are very weak forces between the molecules so they can easily slide over one another – this allows the material to stretch, hence its flexibility. Not much energy is needed to separate the molecules, so rubber has a low melting point.
   b) B, because a lot of energy is needed to separate the strong forces between the molecules.

3. a) Stronger b) Polyethene c) Harder d) Vulcanised rubber
   e) Softer and more flexible f) Children's toys.

4. a) A crystalline polymer is formed by packing the molecules more closely together.
   b) This makes the polymer stronger and more dense, with a slightly higher melting point.

Page 19

1. a) Cradle to Grave.
   b) i) Manufacture ii) Use iii) Disposal.
   c) i) To ensure that the most sustainable method of producing a product is used. Companies are encouraged to reduce waste and be aware of environmental impact. New laws were put in place to protect the environment, cash incentives were given for recycling, and in 1996 a tax was introduced to discourage the use of landfill sites.
      ii) **Accept any other suitable answers.**
      Phase 1: Resources and energy needed to make the product; Environmental impact of making the product from the material.
      Phase 2: Energy needed to use the product, e.g. fuel and electricity; Energy and chemicals needed to maintain the product.
      Phase 3: Energy needed to dispose of the product; Environmental impact of landfill, incineration and recycling.

2. **Accept any other suitable answer.**
   Paper towels. They use less resources and energy than the hand drier in all three phases. However, there is an environmental impact of using paper towels, so environmentally friendly options, e.g. making recyclable towels, should be looked into.

3. a) Teflon.
   b) i)–iii) In any order. Accept any other suitable answers.
   i) Gaskets and valves **ii)** Atomic bombs **iii)** Non-stick saucepans.

Page 20

1. a) i)–iii) In any order.
   i) Landfill sites **ii)** Incineration **iii)** Recycling.
   b) i)–iii) In any order.
   i) Environmental impact **ii)** Cost **iii)** Loss of raw materials.

2. a) ii, iii, v
   b) Non-biodegradable materials waste valuable resources because nothing is being reused or returned to the environment.

3. Accept any other suitable answers.
   Advantage: generates electricity; **Disadvantage:** if too much gas builds up underground it can cause an explosion.

4. a) Burning materials.
   b) Incineration causes air pollution.

5. a) True **b)** False **c)** False **d)** False.

Page 21

1. a) i) Manufacture.
   ii) What method of transportation is required and how does it affect the environment?
   iii) What pollutants are produced during manufacture and transportation?
   iv) To package the nappies?
   v) To transport the nappies between the factory, shop and the consumer's home?
   vi) Disposal.
   vii) Would incineration produce pollutants / toxic gases?
   viii) How much energy could be reclaimed through incineration?
   ix) What is the value of materials and energy wasted when the nappies are thrown away?
   x) How much landfill do the nappies generate?
   b) If a material is very expensive to produce because the manufacturer would not be able to justify producing it at a very high cost.

Page 22

1.

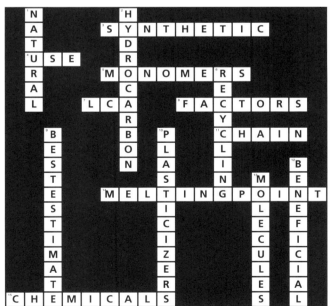

Page 23

1. a) i) Amino acids and proteins.
   ii) They are needed for plants and animals to grow.
   b) The nitrogen cycle shows how nitrogen and its compounds are recycled in nature. It shows the continual cycle of elements through consumption of living organisms and decay.

c) Stage 1: Nitrate salts are absorbed from the soil by plant roots and are used to make proteins.
   Stage 2: Animals eat plants to produce protein containing this same nitrogen.
   Stage 3: Plants and animals die and decay releasing ammonium compounds into the soil.
   Stage 4: Denitrifying bacteria break down nitrates and ammonium compounds in the soil releasing nitrates back into the soil.

Page 24

1. d)

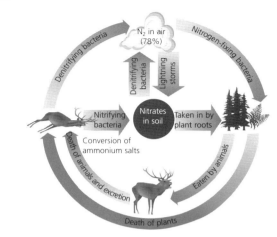

2. a) i)–ii) In any order. Accept any other suitable answers.
   i) Use fertilisers, pesticides and herbicides.
   ii) Keep animals in controlled environments where temperature and movement are limited.
   b) i) Intensive farming.
   ii) Accept any other suitable answer.
      Some people do not think it is morally acceptable as animals have a poor quality of life.
   c) i) Accept any other suitable answers.
      Advantage: More natural methods, so there is not such an environmental impact.
      Disadvantage: Higher costs – more farm workers have to be employed.
   ii) Farms have to pass the UK National and International Standards.
   iii) Soil Association.

Page 25

1. a) i) Replacing lost nitrogen compounds and nutrients in the soil after crops have been harvested.
   ii) Pesticides (chemicals to kill the pests).
   iii) Low yields at higher costs – organic farms are labour intensive.
   iv) High yields at low cost.
   v) Environment.
   vi) Small – less destruction of **hedgerows**.
      Use of natural fertilisers and biological control of pests mean that **food chains** are not affected by chemicals.
   vii) **Hedgerows** often removed to create larger fields and maximise crops planted.
      Use of fertilisers can lead to **eutrophication** and pesticides can harm other organisms that are not pests.
      Pesticides can accumulate in **food chains**.
      A lot of the energy used to make fertilisers depends on burning **fossil fuels**.

Page 26

1. b) Organic.
   c) Accept any suitable answer. Should refer to economic or social costs and crop yields.

2. a) Carbohydrate.
   b) Carbon, hydrogen and oxygen.
   c) $C_6H_{12}O_6$
   d) i) They form starch by joining together in a long chain.

| Individual sugar molecules (glucose) | Huge, long chains of identical sugar molecules (starch). |

ii) The glucose molecules form long chains which are cross-linked.

Individual sugar molecules (glucose)

Long cross-linked chains of sugar molecules (cellulose).

e) Carbon, hydrogen, oxygen, nitrogen, and sometimes other elements such as sulfur.

Page 27

1. a) Sweetener **b)** Colouring **c)** Antioxidant
d) Emulsifier and stabiliser **e)** Preservative **f)** Flavouring.

2. a) That the additive has passed a safety test and is safe to use in the UK and the rest of the European Union.
b) i)–ii) In any order. Accept any other suitable answers.
i) Monosodium glutamate (E621).
ii) Sodium Benzoate (E211).
c) i)–iii) In any order. Accept any other suitable answers.
i) Hyperactivity.
ii) Sleep patterns.
iii) Ability to concentrate.

Page 28

1. a) i)–ii) Accept any other suitable answers.
i) Fruit.
ii) Cassava.
b) i) Gluten.
ii) It can damage the small intestine.
c) i) Moulds growing on cereals, dried fruit and nuts can produce a carcinogenic called aflatoxin.
ii) The chemicals sprayed onto crops may remain in the products we eat.
iii) May produce harmful chemicals.
iv) May result in contamination of bacteria, which can lead to food poisoning.
d) Organic.
e) i)–iii) In any order. Accept any other suitable answers.
i) Have a hygienic kitchen and dispose of waste food quickly.
ii) Cook food properly.
iii) Do not refreeze previously frozen meats.

Page 29

1. a) Independent food safety watchdog set up by an Act of Parliament in 2000.
b) i)–iii) In any order. Accept any other suitable answers.
i) Makes sure that food producers act within the law.
ii) Promotes healthy eating.
iii) Aims to minimise illnesses like food poisoning.
c) Food labels provide a full list of ingredients which help people to decide whether or not to buy a product. For example, coeliacs look for labels that say 'gluten free'.
d) By employing people to carry out research into food issues, e.g. genetically modified (GM) foods.
e) i)–iv) In any order.
i) If the food contains chemicals that could cause harm.
ii) How harmful the chemicals are.
iii) How much of the food must be eaten before it is likely to harm people.
iv) If any groups of people are particularly vulnerable, e.g. the elderly or children, or those suffering from a previous illness.
f) i) If scientific evidence is uncertain and the risk is unknown.
ii) They don't know enough about these foods and the potential health problems they can cause. Their priority has to be to protect public safety and not just let new foods be mass produced and put on the market.

Page 30

1. a)

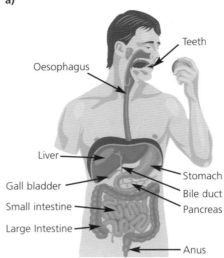

Teeth
Oesophagus
Liver
Gall bladder
Small intestine
Large Intestine
Stomach
Bile duct
Pancreas
Anus

b) The breaking down of large insoluble molecules into smaller soluble molecules using enzymes.
c) To make the molecules small and soluble enough to diffuse through the small intestine walls and into the blood, where they can be transported to different parts of the body.
d) i)–ii) In any order.
i) Kills bacteria.
ii) Provides the best conditions for the enzyme to help digest food.
e) It is carried to the stomach by the oesophagus. In the stomach it is stored and mixed with an enzyme and acid to help digest it and kill any bacteria. Further enzymes complete the digestion in the small intestine, from where the small soluble molecules are then absorbed into the bloodstream. In the large intestine, excess water is removed and faeces stored.
f) i) They are transported to the liver where they are broken down to form urea. Urea is transported in the blood to the kidneys where it is filtered out before being excreted in urine.
ii) During the breakdown of the amino acids, harmful chemicals are formed.

Page 31

1. a) i) Carbohydrates **ii)** Bread **iii)** Eggs **iv)** Meat **v)** Fish **vi)** Fruit **vii)** Vegetables **viii)** Fats **ix)** Fibre.
b) Fatty, sugary foods.
c) Eating too much and not exercising enough.
d) i)–iii) In any order. Accept any other suitable answers.
i) Foods that contain a lot of fat, salt and sugar often taste good.
ii) Processed microwave meals are quick and easy.
iii) Fruit and vegetables can be expensive to buy.
e) i)–iii) In any order.
i) Heart disease **ii)** Cancer **iii)** Diabetes.
f) i)–ii) In either order. Accept any other suitable answers.
i) Exercise more.
ii) Eat fruit as a snack rather than crisps or sweets.

Page 32

1. a) Diabetes is a disease caused by the pancreas not producing and releasing enough insulin, which means the blood sugar level fluctuates.
b) Many processed foods, which contain high levels of sugar, and are quickly absorbed into the bloodstream.
c) The pancreas releases insulin. Glucose from the blood is converted to insoluble glycogen in the liver and is removed from the blood. The blood glucose concentration then returns to normal.
d) Type 1 diabetes: The pancreas stops producing insulin altogether as the special cells in the pancreas are destroyed. **Treatment:** Injecting insulin.
Type 2 diabetes: The pancreas does not make enough insulin or the cells do not respond. **Treatment:** Diet and exercise, although medicine and insulin injections are usually also needed.
e) More young people are becoming obese and are therefore at a higher risk.
f) Risk factors.

Page 33

1.

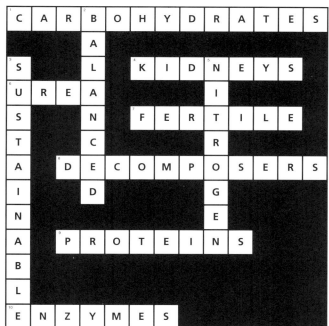

Crossword grid:
- 1 across: CARBOHYDRATES
- 2 down: BALANCED
- 3 down: SUSTAINABLE
- 4 across: KIDNEYS
- 5 down: FIBRE
- 6 across: UREA
- 7 across: FERTILE
- 8 down: DECOMPOSERS / DD
- 9 across: PROTEINS
- 10 across: ENZYMES

Page 34

1. a) About 100.
   b) i) A group.
      ii) **Accept any other suitable answers.**
          Magnesium (Mg), Calcium (Ca), Radium (Ra)
      iii) Elements in the same group have the same number of electrons in their outermost shell.
      iv) 4
   c) i) A period.
      ii) **Accept any other suitable answers.**
          Potassium (K), Calcium (Ca), Scandium (Sc)
      iii) They are the same.
      iv) **Silver: 5 Tin: 5**
   d) i) Hf
      ii) 178
      iii) 72

Page 35

1. a)

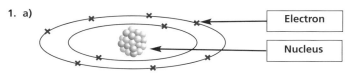

Electron

Nucleus

   b) i) +1. Positively charged.
      ii) Zero. Neutral.
      iii) -1. Negatively charged.
      iv) Zero. No electrical charge because an atom has the same number of protons as electrons.
   c) i) 1
      ii) 1
      iii) 0 (nearly). Negligible, i.e. nearly nothing, compared to a proton or neutron.

2. a) i) Red ii) Yellow iii) Lilac.
   b) An energy change as excited electrons fall from high energy levels to lower ones.
   c) It has helped chemists to discover new elements.

Page 36

1. a) Electronic configuration tells us how electrons are arranged around the nucleus of an atom in shells (energy levels).
   b) i) The first shell has a maximum of 2 electrons. The shells after that have a maximum of 8 electrons.
      ii) Potassium is in Group 1 (number of electrons in outermost shell).
      iii) It is in the fourth period (number of energy levels occupied by electrons equals the number of the period).

2. a) 2.8.8.2 b) 2.1 c) 2.3 d) 2.8.7

Page 37

1. The products of a chemical reaction are made up from exactly the same atoms as the reactants – no atoms are lost or made.

2. a) Nitrogen monoxide + Carbon monoxide $\longrightarrow$ Nitrogen + Carbon dioxide
   b) That two molecules of nitrogen monoxide gas and two molecules of carbon monoxide gas produce one molecule of nitrogen gas and two molecules of carbon dioxide gas.

3. a) $Cu + O_2 \longrightarrow CuO$
   b) **Accept any suitable diagrams.**
      There are 2 Os on the reactant side but only 1 O on the product side. So we need to add another CuO to the product side to balance the Os. Therefore, we also need to add another Cu on the reactant side to balance the Cus.
      There are now 2 Cu atoms and 2 O atoms on each side which means the equation is balanced.
   c) $2Cu(s) + O_2(g) \longrightarrow 2CuO(s)$

Page 38

1. a Corrosive; they attack living tissue, including eyes and skin, and can damage materials.
   b) Oxidising; these substances provide oxygen, which allows other substances to burn more fiercely.
   c) Toxic; these substances can kill when swallowed, breathed in or absorbed through the skin.

2. a) Do not work near a naked flame.
   b) i)–ii) **Accept any other suitable answers.**
      i) Wear eye protection and gloves.
      ii) Wash hands after handling chemicals.

3. a) 6
   b) i) Their boiling points decrease.
      ii) They become more reactive.
      iii) Their density increases.
   c) i) Floats and melts – gentle reaction. Lithium hydroxide and hydrogen gas are formed.
      ii) Vigorous reaction to form lithium chloride.
      iii) Vigorous reaction to form sodium chloride.
      iv) Quickly tarnishes and becomes covered in a layer of potassium oxide.
      v) Floats and melts – very aggressive reaction, so much so that it catches fire. Potassium hydroxide and hydrogen gas are formed.
      vi) Vigorous reaction to form potassium chloride.

Page 39

4. a) i) Potassium + Chlorine $\longrightarrow$ Potassium chloride
      ii) Lithium + Water $\longrightarrow$ Lithium hydroxide + Hydrogen
      iii) Sodium + Oxygen $\longrightarrow$ Sodium oxide
   b) ii) LiOH iii) Na_2O

5. a) $4M(s) + O_2(g) = 2M_2O(s)$
   b) $2M(s) + 2H_2O(l) = 2MOH(aq) + H_2(g)$

6. a) i)–iii) **In any order. Accept any other suitable answers.**
      i) Use small amounts of very dilute concentrations.
      ii) Wear safety glasses and use safety screens.
      iii) Watch teacher demonstrations.
   b) Put universal indicator into a beaker of water. Universal indicator should be green to show neutral pH. Put a small piece of sodium into the beaker. Sodium reacts with water and gives off hydrogen gas. When it has finished reacting, the beaker contains sodium hydroxide solution. The solution should now be purple showing it is alkaline.

Page 40

1. a) 5
   b) i) Their boiling points increase.
      ii) They become less reactive.
      iii) Their density increases.

2. a) A molecule that exists in pairs of atoms.
   b) i)–ii) **Accept any other suitable answers.**
      i) Cl_2
      ii) I_2

3. **a)** Sterilising water, making pesticides and plastics **b)** HCl **c)** NaCl
   d) Orange liquid **e)** HBr **f)** NaBr **g)** Grey solid **h)** Antiseptic to sterilise wounds **i)** NaI

4. Displacement reaction.

Page 41

1. **a)** They have the same number of electrons in their outermost shell. In Group 1, the highest occupied energy level contains 1 electron. In Group 7, the highest occupied energy level contains 7 electrons.
   b) The outermost electron shell gets further away from the influence of the nucleus and so an electron is more easily lost.
   c) The outermost electron shell gets further away from the influence of the nucleus and so an electron is less easily gained.

2. **a)** Negative and positive electrodes are placed in an electrolyte solution. A power supply is connected to the electrodes and the positive particles are attracted to the negative electrodes whilst the negative particles are attracted to the positive electrode.
   b) Ions

3. **a)** An ion is formed when an atom loses or gains one or more electrons and it carries an overall charge because the proton and electron numbers are no longer equal.
   b) A cation is when an ion has been formed by an atom losing an electron(s) and it has an overall positive charge, because it now has more protons than electrons.
   An anion is when an ion has been formed by an atom gaining an electron(s) and it has an overall negative charge, because it now has more electrons than protons.

Page 42

1. Group 1 and Group 7

2. The K atom has 1 electron in its outer shell which is transferred to the chlorine atom, so they both have 8 electrons in their outer shell. The atoms become K^+ and Cl^- and the compound formed is potassium chloride or KCl.

3. A giant crystal lattice

4.

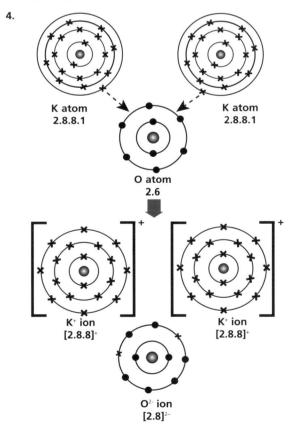

K atom
2.8.8.1

K atom
2.8.8.1

O atom
2.6

K⁺ ion
[2.8.8]⁺

K⁺ ion
[2.8.8]⁺

O²⁻ ion
[2.8]²⁻

Page 43

5. The Ca atom has 2 electrons in its outer shell which is transferred to the O atom, so they both have 8 electrons in their outer shell. The atoms become Ca^{2+} and O^{2-}, and the compound formed is calcium oxide, CaO.

6. There is a strong force of attraction between the ions, which takes a lot of energy to break, leading to high melting and boiling points. When the compound is molten or dissolved, the charged ions are free to move around the liquid, so they can conduct electricity.

7. **a) i)** LiOH **ii)** 2LiO **iii)** Al_2O_3
   b) i) 2⁺ **ii)** 2⁺ **iii)** 6⁺

Page 44

1. **a)** Biosphere **b)** Atmosphere **c) i)** Hydrosphere **ii)** Lithosphere

I	A	B	L	E	S	U	T	F	O	W	T	M
C	W	G	X	C	S	L	G	A	N	H	N	E
O	A	S	A	M	E	A	V	G	Y	T	M	L
M	T	V	O	B	R	E	W	D	R	E	P	E
P	M	T	Y	I	T	T	R	S	O	R	E	V
O	O	I	L	O	I	O	T	L	D	F	C	V
U	S	H	U	S	S	N	C	A	X	C	V	P
N	P	B	K	P	E	D	P	C	Z	B	N	Y
D	H	F	H	H	U	R	N	I	Q	W	L	O
S	E	E	E	E	D	F	R	M	C	X	Z	A
R	R	F	Y	R	P	G	S	E	T	Y	E	C
E	E	R	Y	E	G	A	S	H	R	J	K	L
I	L	I	T	H	O	S	P	H	E	R	E	S
P	R	O	P	E	R	T	I	E	S	T	W	Y

2. **a)–c) In any order.**
   a) Silicon, (Si) **b)** Oxygen, (O) **c)** Aluminium, (Al)

3. **a)–d) In any order.**
   a) Carbon, (C) **b)** Hydrogen, (H) **c)** Oxygen, (O) **d)** Nitrogen, (N)

Page 45

1. **a)–b) In any order.**
   a) Nitrogen **b)** Carbon

2. The carbon cycle is the continual recycling of carbon in nature. For example, carbon dioxide is moved by green plants during photosynthesis, into the biosphere, and is then returned to the atmosphere during respiration.

3. **a)** Lithosphere
   b) Nitrogen is returned to the lithosphere.
   c) By denitrifying bacteria.

4. Burning fossil fuels.

Page 46

1. **a)–e) In any order.**
   a) Oxygen **b)** Nitrogen **c)** Carbon dioxide **d)** Water vapour
   e) Argon

2. **a)** It tells us that they are gases.
   b) They are small molecules with weak forces of attraction between them. Only small amounts of energy are needed to break these forces, which allow the molecules to move freely through the air.
   c) No charge – when pure they do not conduct electricity.
   d) i) They are connected by strong covalent bonds.
   ii) There is an electrostatic attraction between the nuclei of the atoms and the shared pair of electrons. **Accept any suitable diagram showing shared electrons between the nuclei.**

Pages 47

1. It contains dissolved ionic compounds called 'salts'.

2. a)–c) In any order. Accept any other suitable answers.
   a) Sodium chloride.
   b) Magnesium sulfate.
   c) Potassium chloride.

3. It has a much higher boiling point than all of the other small molecules in the hydrosphere.

4. It is bent, because the electrons in the covalent bond are nearer the oxygen atom than the hydrogen atoms. There are small charges on the atoms which mean that the forces between the molecules are slightly stronger than in other covalent molecules. More energy is therefore needed to separate them.

5. The small charges on the atoms. They attract the charges on the ions; the ions can then break away and move freely through the liquid.

6. a) Silicon dioxide.
   b) i)–iv) In any order.
   i) Very hard **ii)** High melting and boiling points **iii)** Electrical insulator **iv)** Insoluble in water

Page 48

7. a)–b) In any order.
   a) Quartz **b)** Sandstone

8. a) There are no free electrons or ions to carry the electrical charge.
   b) A lot of energy is needed to break the strong covalent bond between the atoms.

9. a)–c) In any order.
   a) Carbohydrates **b)** Proteins **c)** DNA

10. Glucose contains carbon, hydrogen and oxygen.

11. a) Fat 2 **b)** DNA **c)** Protein

Page 49

1. a) The mass of the reactants is equal to the mass of the products, so there are the same numbers of atoms on both sides of the equation.

   b) i)–ii) In any order.
   i) Write a number in front of one or more of the formulae. This increases the number of all of the atoms in the formula.
   ii) Remember to include the state symbols.

2. a) $Cu(s) + O_2(g) \longrightarrow CuO(s)$
   b) Because there are more oxygen atoms on the reactants side.
   c) $2Cu(s) + O_2(g) \longrightarrow 2CuO(s)$

3. a) It is a number that compares the mass of one atom to the mass of other atoms.
   b) A_r
   c) i) The larger of the two (at the top of the symbol).
   ii) The mass number.

Page 50

1. a) Minerals
   b) A rock that contains varying amounts of minerals from which metals can be extracted.

2. a) They are very reactive metals and so energy is required to extract them from their ores.
   b) Electrolysis
   c) i) Carbon
   ii) They are extracted by heating with carbon / carbon monoxide.
   d) i)–ii) In any order.
   i) Gold **ii)** Platinum

3. a) In 100g of CuO there will be $\frac{63.5}{79.5} \times 100 = 79.9$g of Cu

   b) Relative formula mass: $(2 \times 79.5) + 12 = (2 \times 63.5) + 44$
                        $159 + 12 = 127 + 44$
                             $171 = 171$
   Therefore, 159g of CuO produces 127g of Cu

   So, 1g of CuO $= \frac{127}{159} = 0.8$g of Cu

Page 51

1. a) A life cycle analysis.
   b) i) Extraction **ii)** Use **iii)** Disposal

© Letts and Lonsdale

---

2. a) i)–ii) In any order.
   i) Energy use **ii)** Transport
   b) i)–iii) In any order.
   i) Reuse **ii)** Recycle **iii)** Throw away

3. a) The decomposition of an electrolyte (solution that conducts electricity) with an electric current.
   b) In industry to extract metals from their ores.

4. The ions have to be free to move – this happens when it is either molten or dissolved in solution.

5. The positively charged ions (in this case, lead) are attracted to the negative electrode. The negatively charged ions (bromide) are attracted to the positive electrode.

6. a) Discharged.
   b) It means that the ions lose their charge.

Page 52

1. a) It is too reactive to be extracted by heating with carbon.
   b) Purified aluminium oxide and cryolite (a compound of aluminium) to lower its melting point.
   c) It is melted.
   d) i) The positively charged aluminium ions move towards the negative cathode and aluminium is formed.
   ii) Negatively charged oxygen ions move towards the positive electrode and oxygen is formed.
   e) Large amounts of electrical energy are needed to carry out the extraction and this is expensive.
   f) $2Al_2O_3(l) \longrightarrow 4Al(l) + 3O_2(g)$
   g) $Al^{3+}(l) + 3e^- \xrightarrow{reduction} Al(l)$
   h) $2O^{2-}(l) - 4e^- \xrightarrow{oxidation} O_2(g)$

Page 53

1. a) i)–iv) In any order.
   i) Strong **ii)** Malleable **iii)** High melting point **iv)** Conduct electricity
   b) i)–iv) In any order.
   i) Strong. Metal ions are closely packed in a lattice structure.
   ii) Malleable. External forces cause layers of metal ions to move by sliding over other layers.
   iii) High melting point. A lot of energy is needed to break the strong force of attraction between the metal ions and the sea of electrons.
   iv) Conduct electricity. Electrons are free to move throughout the structure. When an electrical force is applied, the electrons move along the metal in one direction.
   c) Accept any other suitable answers.
   i) Conducts heat **ii)** Electrical switches **iii)** Iron **iv)** High melting point **v)** Aluminium **vi)** Malleable **vii)** Lightweight **viii)** Lightweight **ix)** Bicycles **x)** Submarines

Page 54

1. a)–e) In any order. Accept any other suitable answers.
   a) Pharmaceuticals **b)** Cosmetics **c)** Fertilisers **d)** Paints
   e) Industrial glass

2. a) Bulk chemicals.
   b) i)–ii) In any order.
   i) Sulfuric acid **ii)** Ammonia

3. a) A small scale.
   b) i)–ii) In any order.
   i) Drugs **ii)** Pesticides
   c) Because many of them can be hazardous and you need to learn about the necessary precautions that should be taken.

4. a) A measure of the acidity or alkalinity of an aqueous solution across a 14-point scale.
   b) i) An acid is a substance that has a pH of less than 7.
   ii) An alkali is a soluble base (a base being the oxides and hydroxides of metals) that has a pH of more than 7.

Page 55

5. a) i) Neutral **ii)** Very acidic **iii)** Very alkaline **iv)** Slightly acidic
   v) Slightly alkaline
   b) i)–iii) Accept any other suitable answers.
   i) Hydrochloric acid **ii)** Water **iii)** Dilute sodium hydroxide

c) It is measured using an indicator such as universal indicator solution or a pH meter.

6. a) i) Sodium hydroxide **ii)** Alkali
  b) i) Sulfuric acid **ii)** Acid
  c) i) Calcium hydroxide **ii)** Alkali
  d) i) Hydrochloric acid (hydrogen chloride) **ii)** Acid
  e) i) Potassium hydroxide **ii)** Alkali

7. a) Aqueous hydrogen ions (H^+ (aq))
  b) Aqueous hydroxide ions (OH^-(aq))

Page 56

1. a) Neutralisation is where an acid and a base are mixed together in the correct amounts and 'cancel' each other out.
  b) 7
  c) Acid + Base $\longrightarrow$ Neutral salt solution + Water
  d) H^+(aq)$+ OH^-$(aq)$\longrightarrow H_2O$(l)

2. a) i)–ii) In any order.
    i) The metal in the base **ii)** The acid used
  b) i) Chloride salts **ii)** Sulfate salts **iii)** Nitrate salts

3. a) Copper sulfate.
  b) NaC(aq)
  c) Potassium nitrate
  d) $Ca(NO_3)_2$(aq)

Page 57

1. a i)–iii) In any order.
    i) NaCl **ii)** KCl **iii)** Na_2CO_3
  b) i) Na = 1+, Cl = 1-
    ii) K = 1+, Cl = 1-
    iii) Na_2 = 2+, CO_3 = 2-

2. a) i)–iii) In any order. Accept any other suitable answers.
    i) $MgSO_4$ **ii)** $MgCO_3$ **iii)** $CaCl_2$
  b) Answers included for salts listed above. Accept correct answers for other suitable salts.
    i) Mg = 2+, SO_4 = 2-
    ii) Mg = 2+, CO_3 = 2-
    iii) Ca = 2+, Cl_2 = 2-

3. a)–d) In any order.
  a) Chlorine, Cl_2 **b)** Hydrogen, H_2 **c)** Nitrogen, N_2 **d)** Oxygen, O_2

4. a) More of it is formed.
  b) Percentage yield = $\dfrac{\text{Actual yield}}{\text{Theoretical yield}}$ x 100

Page 58

5. a) Answer given b) Risk assessment **c)** Temperature **d)** Product **e)** Purify **f)** Yield **g)** Purity.

6. a) Zinc + Hydrochloric acid $\longrightarrow$ Zinc chloride + Hydrogen
  b) Wear safety glasses; zinc chloride is corrosive so it is harmful if inhaled or swallowed. Do not allow it to come in contact with your skin; wear protective gloves. Ensure that there is adequate ventilation.
  c) Filter it using a paper filter and a funnel.
  d) 10%

Page 59

1. a)–c) Accept three of the following: relative atomic mass; relative formula mass; that a balanced equation shows the number of atoms / molecules taking part in the reaction; how to work out the ratio of mass of reactant to mass of product; how to apply the ratio to the question.

2. a) i) 27 **ii)** 35 **iii)** 14 **iv)** 40 **v)** 73
  b) The mass number.

3. a) i) The relative atomic masses of all its elements added together.
    ii) M_r
  b) i)–ii) In any order.
    i) Formula of the compound.
    ii) Relative atomic mass of all the atoms involved.
  c) i) 159 **ii)** 98 **iii)** 17

Page 60

1. a) i) 100 **ii)** 72 **iii)** 110 **iv)** 44 **v)** 18
  b) 172
  c) 172
  d) Yes. There is no loss of mass in a chemical reaction.
  e) 2.2g

2. 0.91kg / 909g

Page 61

1. a) Titrations can be used to calculate the purity of an acid by neutralising the acid with a known amount of alkali.
  b) i) Burette, alkali.
    ii) Distilled water.
    iii) Pipette, acid.
    iv) Indicator, colourless, burette.
    v) Alkali, burette.
    vi) Repeat, same.

2. Divide by 1000.

3. a) 3 x the volume and concentration of the alkali divided by the volume of citric acid.
  b) Mass = Concentration x Value
  c) $\dfrac{\text{Calculated mass}}{\text{Mass weighed out at start}}$ x 100

Page 62

1. a) They collide with each other with sufficient energy to react.
  b) i)–ii) Accept any other suitable answers.
    i) Rusting **ii)** Burning

2. a)–c) In any order.
  a) Measure the amount of reactants used.
  b) Measure the amount of products used.
  c) Observe or measure the formation of a precipitate / colour change.

3. a) X. The line is steeper than Y and therefore the reaction is faster.
  b) i)–iii) Accept three of the following: Surface area of solid reactants in Reaction X is greater than in Reaction Y; temperature of Reaction X is greater than Reaction Y; a catalyst is used in Reaction X but not in Reaction Y; concentration of solution in Reaction X is greater than in Reaction Y.
  c) That one of the reactants is used up and the reaction has stopped.
  d) The same amount of product is formed from the same amount of reactants.

Page 63

1. a)–d) In any order.
  a) Temperature
  b) Particle size or surface area.
  c) Concentration
  d) Use of a catalyst.

2. a) They move quite slowly and do not collide that often, so fewer collisions are successful.
  b) When a mixture is heated, the particles move more quickly and collide with each other more often and with greater energy, so more collisions are successful.

3. a) Particles are spread out – they collide with each other less often resulting in fewer successful collisions.
  b) Particles are crowded close together – particles collide with each other more often, resulting in many more successful collisions.

4.

	Surface area	Collisions	Reaction rate
Large particles	Small	Few	Slow
Small particles	Large	Many	Fast

5. A catalyst is a substance which increases the rate of a chemical reaction without being changed itself during the process.

Page 64

6. a) Slowly **b)** Fizzing

7 a) They move a lot faster.

b) There are many more energetic collisions and they happen more frequently. This means that the minimum energy required for a reaction will occur more often, leading to a greater rate of reaction.

c) More frequent collisions and more collisions that are sufficiently energetic for a reaction to happen.

8. Lowers the amount of energy needed for a successful collision.

9. It is not used up during the reaction so can be used again and again.

10. a)–c) Accept any other suitable answers.

a) Carry out a complete risk assessment of the chemical synthesis and take the necessary precautions, e.g. buying necessary safety equipment.

b) Must have a high enough rate of manufacture to produce a sufficient daily yield.

c) Does the chemical synthesis produce any harmful by-products that have an impact on the environment?

Page 65

1. a)–b) In any order: carbon; hydrogen

2. Single carbon–carbon bonds.

3. Because there are no spare bonds left / they are all single bonds.

4.

Name of Hydrocarbon	Formula	Structural Formula
Propane	C_3H_8	H H H | | | H–C–C–C–H | | | H H H
Butane	C_4H_{10}	H H H H | | | | H–C–C–C–C–H | | | | H H H H
Ethane	C_2H_6	H H | | H–C–C–H | | H H

5. Because they are not polar and water molecules cannot get between their molecules.

6. a) 2; 2
b) 2; 7; 4; 6

Page 66

7. –OH

8.

$$\begin{array}{cc} H & H \\ | & | \\ H-C-C-O-H \\ | & | \\ H & H \end{array}$$

9. a)–c) In any order: solvent; fuel; component in alcoholic drinks.

10. a)–b) Accept any two from: chemical feedstock; fuels; adhesives; foams; cosmetics; solvents.

11. The carbon atoms combine with oxygen to form carbon dioxide. The hydrogen atoms combine with oxygen to form water.

12. Sodium reacts slowly and steadily gives off bubbles of hydrogen. Sodium ethoxide is formed. The sodium sinks in the ethanol.

© Letts and Lonsdale

13. Sodium propoxide

14. False

Page 67

1. a)–b) In any order: the taste of rancid butter; the aroma of sweaty feet.

2. –COOH

3.

Name of Hydrocarbon	Formula	Structural Formula
Ethanoic acid	CH_3CO_2H	H O | // H–C–C | \\ H O–H

Methanoic acid	HCO_2H	O
		   //
		H–C
		   \\
		  O–H

4. a) Sodium ethanoate
b) Ethanoic acid; water
c) Sodium carbonate; water

5. lard; saturated; unreactive; single; unsaturated; reactive; double; energy

Page 68

1. Ethanol; Water

2. a) ii) Sweet smell
b) i)–iii) In any order: perfumes; fragrances; food products

3. a) Continuous heating or continuous boiling.
b) It is added because it is a catalyst and so it speeds up the reaction.

4. To remove or separate the ester.

5. a)

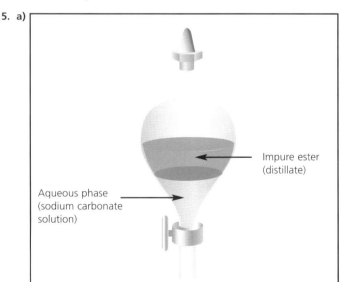

Impure ester (distillate)

Aqueous phase (sodium carbonate solution)

b) So it will react with any remaining acid and extract it into the aqueous phase.

6. a) It removes any remaining water molecules.
b) Filtration

Page 69

1. a) Carbon + Oxygen ⟶ Carbon dioxide + Heat Energy
b) Exothermic
c) Accept any suitable answer, e.g.: neutralising alkalis with acids.

2. a) Energy is taken in from the surroundings.
b) They are accompanied by a fall in temperature.
c) Accept any suitable answer, e.g.: dissolving nitrate crystals in water.

3. a) Bonds in the reactants are broken and new bonds between the atoms are made so products are formed.

b) False, breaking a chemical reaction is an endothermic reaction so it takes in a lot of energy.

4. a) It is the energy needed to start a reaction and break old bonds.

b)

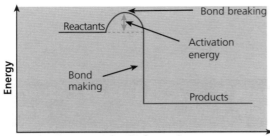

Progress of Reaction

Page 70

1. a) 4 x C-H = 4 x 412 = 1648
2 x O = 0 = 2 x 496 = 992
Total = 2640kJ

b) 2 x C = 0 = 2 x 743 = 1486
4 x O-H = 4 x 463 = 1852
Total = 3338

c) i) Energy change = 2640 – 3338 = 698kJ
ii) To predict the energy changes / to know if a reaction is going to be suitable for what they need it to do.

d) Exothermic because the energy from making the products is more than that needed to break bonds in the reactants.

e)

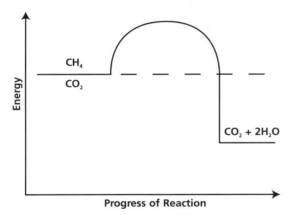

Progress of Reaction

Page 71

1. a) It means that it is a reversible reaction.
b) The solid ammonium chloride has decomposed into NH_3 and HCl when it was heated.
c) As the gases cool down, the molecules come closer together, react and form ammonium chloride.
d) $NH_4Cl(s) \rightleftharpoons NH_3(g) + HCl(g)$

2. a) A system where no reactants are added and no products are taken away.
b) The concentration of the reactants and products do not change.

3. a) Decrease the temperature.
b) The yield will increase.

Page 72

1. Both the forward and backward reactions are still occurring but at the same rate.

2. At the start: The iodine particles are dissolved in the solvent. **Diagram: All the molecule should be in the top circle**.

Dynamic equilibrium: Particles move between the solvent and solution. **Diagram: the majority of the molecules should be in the top circle, but there should be some in the bottom circle**.

At equilibrium: The particles continue to move, but there is an equal distribution of particles in the solvent and aqueous solution. **Diagram: there should be an even number of molecules in both circles**.

3. a) i)–ii) Accept any two from: hydrochloric acid; nitric acid; sulfuric acid
b) Carboxylic acid
c) In a strong acid, all the molecules are ionised. In a weak acid, only about 1% of the molecules are ionised.

Page 73

1. Qualitative; indicators; thin layer chromatography; quantitative; acid–base titration.

2. To ensure that the samples collected are not contaminated, and so are more reliable. It also means that different people can repeat a test on the same sample.

3. a) It is used to find out what unknown substances are made up of.
b) Model answer: A chromatogram is formed when chemicals come out of solution and bind to the paper. For each component of the sample, a dynamic equilibrium is set up between the stationary phase (paper) and the mobile phase (solvent). Different molecules in the sample travel different distances according to how strongly they are attracted to the molecules in the stationary phase, in relation to their attraction to the solvent molecules.

Page 74

3. c)

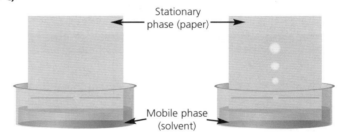

4. a) So there are known substances that the unknown white powder can be compared to.
b) Detergent

5. a) A thin layer of absorbent material, e.g. silica gel; alumina; cellulose.
b) i)–iii) In any order: faster runs; more even movement of the mobile phase; a choice of different absorbencies for the stationary phase.

6. a)–b) In any order: develop the chromatogram by spraying with a chemical that causes coloration; view under UV light and mark spots on plate.

Page 75

1. The movement of a substance relative to the movement of a solvent front.

2. a) i) 0.33 **ii)** 0.67 **iii)** 0.92
b) A table of R_f values to compare the answer to.

3. It is the analysis of samples of liquids, gases or volatile solids, e.g. checking air quality or water quality.

4. A microscopic layer of liquid on an unreactive solid support.

Page 76

5. a)–b) In any order: detecting banned substance in blood and urine samples; analysing the exact characteristics of pesticide spills and matching them to samples from suspected sources.

6. a) It is the time taken for each substance to pass through the chromatographic system.
b) Because different substances have different solubilities.

7. The amount of chemical in a sample.

8. a) 3 **b)** 1 **c)** 4 **d)** 8 **e)** 5 **f)** 7 **g)** 6 **h)** 2

Page 77

1. It is the amount of solid that is dissolved in the liquid.

2. Concentration (g/dm³) = $\dfrac{\text{Mass (g)}}{\text{Volume (dm}^3\text{)}}$

3. Divide the figure in cm³ by 1000.

4. a) 40g/dm³
   b) 440g/dm³

5. a) 4.8g
   b) 55g
   c) 1.25g

6. It is the concentration of a known solution.

Page 78

1. A technique which can be used to find the volume of a liquid needed to neutralise an acid / alkali.

2. a) 7 b) 4 c) 6 d) 1 e) 2 f) 3 g) 5

3. **Accept any suitable answer,** e.g. phenolphthalein

4. So that an average value can be worked out. This should give a more accurate result.

5. pH probe

6. 2g/dm³

Page 79

1. a) 57.5g/dm³
   b) 55.05g/dm³
   c) 55.2g/dm³ – 54.9g/dm³
   d) 0.3g/dm³
   e) 0.55%

2. Systematic; high; incorrectly; random.

3. a) Random b) Systematic c) Systematic d) Systematic

Page 80

1. a)–c) **Any three from:** ammonia; sulfuric acid; sodium hydroxide; phosphoric acid.

2. a)–c) **In any order:** drugs; food additives; fragrances.

3. To protect people and the environment from danger.

4. a) No, it may irritate sensitive skin.
   b) Yes, it has the correct sun protection and does not cause any skin reactions.
   c) Sun cream C has an actual sun protection factor that is lower than advertised. If this was used there is the chance that people could get burnt by the Sun, increasing their risk of getting skin cancer.

Page 81

1. a) By-product b) Atom economy c) Yield d) Brown e) Toxic
   f) Green g) Feedstocks h) Renewable i) Catalyst

2. False

3. False

4. It is the type of development that meets the needs of present generations without compromising future generations.

5. Reduce; faster; unchanged; sustainable

Page 82

1. a) Fractional distillation b) Cracking; catalyst c) Purified
   d) Ethene; feedstock e) Zeolites f) Ethanol g) Unreacted

2. Ethene + Steam $\longrightarrow$ Ethanol

3. $C_2H_4(g) + H_2O(g) \longrightarrow C_2H_5OH(g)$

Page 83

4. a) A reaction in which natural sugars are converted to alcohol by reacting with water and the enzymes in yeast.
   b) Yeast; carbon dioxide

5. a) The enzyme becomes denatured and is no longer able to work.
   b) An enzyme can also become denatured by a change in pH level.

6. a)–b) **In any order:** the amount of sugar in the mixture; the enzymes in the yeast.

7. By distillation

8. a)–c) **In any order:** wood waste; corn stalks; rice hulls

9. The new genes allow the bacteria to digest all the sugars in the biomass and convert them into ethanol.

Page 84

1. a) i)–ii) **In any order:** it has a higher energy use that the other methods; it produces toxic waste and is not carbon neutral.
   b) Biotechnology is the most sustainable. It uses waste products as the raw materials, so new materials need to be produced in order to make the ethanol.

Page 86

1. a) ii
   b) Food Standards Agency
   c) i)–iii) **In any order.** Stabilisers; preservatives; flavourings. **Accept any other suitable answers**.
   d) i)–ii) **In any order.** They are unnecessary as they only have a cosmetic effect; Certain food colourings may be linked to behavioural changes and disorders in children.
   e) i)–iii) **In any order:** Tartrazine, E102; Sunset yellow, E110; Brilliant Blue FCF, E133
   f) By mixing E133 with E102.
   g) They have been found to cause cancer in animals. The FSA does not consider them to be safe.
   h) They recalled any sold items and withdrew any products on sale which contained the dye.

Page 87

Acknowledgements

The author and publisher would like to thank everyone who has contributed to this book:

Front cover ©2007 Jupiterimages Corporation
Inside Front Cover ©iStockphoto.com / Andrei Tchernov

ISBN 978-1-906415-05-1

Published by Letts and Lonsdale

©2008 Lonsdale, a division of Huveaux Plc.

Author: Dorothy Warren

Editors: Charlotte Christensen and Tracy Cowell

Cover and Concept Design: Sarah Duxbury

Designer: Joanne Hatfield

Letts and Lonsdale make every effort to ensure that all paper used in our books is made from wood pulp obtained from well-managed forests, controlled sources and recycled wood or fibre.

Author Information

Dr Dorothy Warren, is a member of the Royal Society of Chemistry, a former science teacher, and a Secondary Science Consultant with the Quality and Improvement Service for North Yorkshire County Council. Having been involved in the pilot scheme for OCR Twenty First Century Science, she has an excellent understanding of the new specifications, which she has helped to implement in local schools.

This answer book should be used to mark students' responses to the questions in
OCR Twenty First Century GCSE Chemistry Revision Plus Student Workbook

978-1-905896-99-8

Ordering Details

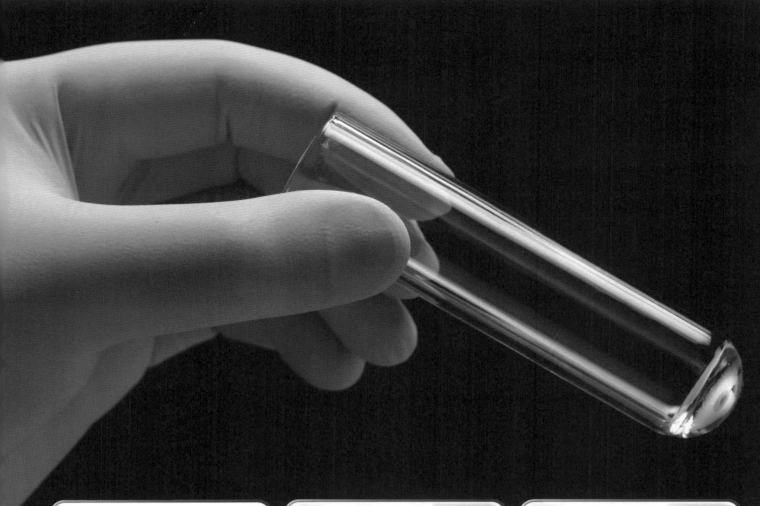

INFORMATION

For up-to-date product information, including prices, please visit our website or telephone our customer services department:

Web: www.lettsandlonsdale.com
Enquiries: 015395 65921

SCHOOLS

Educational providers can order online and by fax, telephone or post:

Letts and Lonsdale
PO BOX 113, Holme,
Carnforth, LA6 1WL

Order Line: 015395 64910
Fax: 015395 64167
Web: www.lettsandlonsdale.com

PRIVATE CUSTOMERS

Secure ordering is available online at
www.lettsandlonsdale.com

www.lettsandlonsdale.com
Browse for a full list of publications and further information